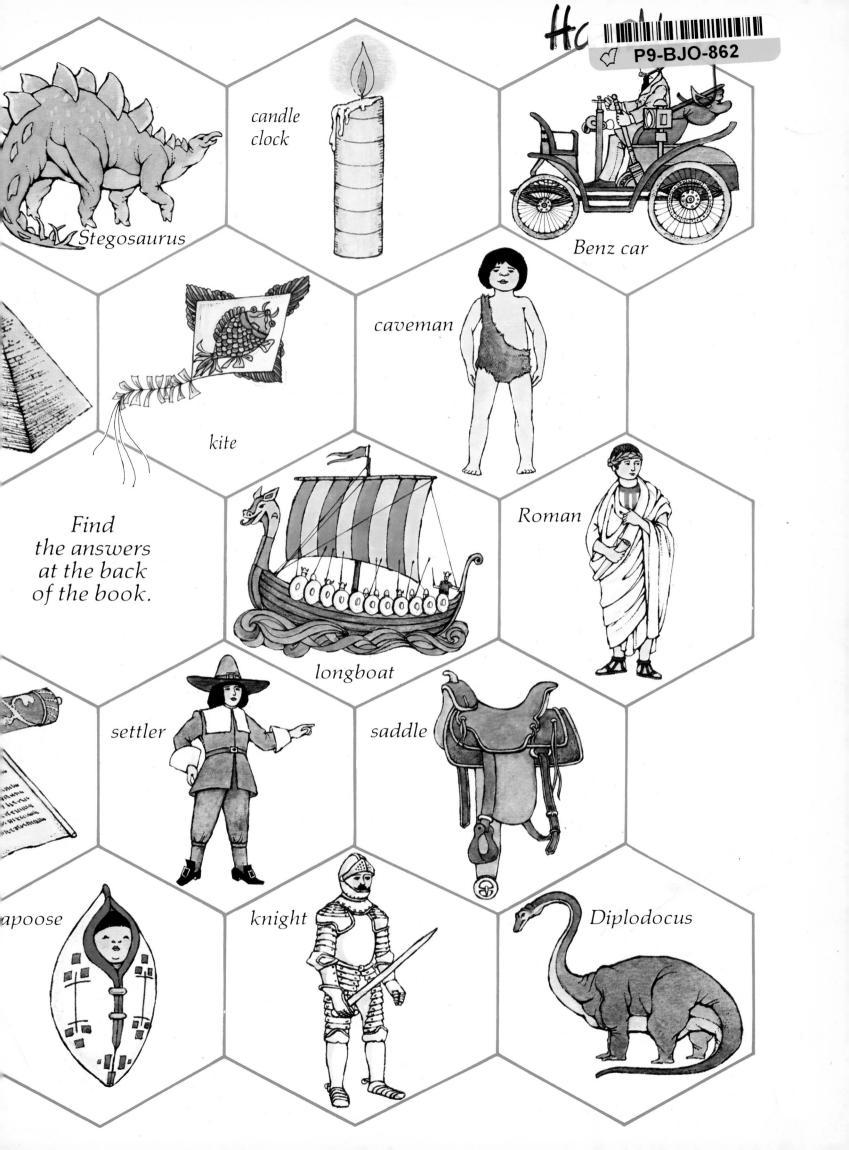

Stegosaurus

candle
clock

Benz car

caveman

kite

Roman

Find
the answers
at the back
of the book.

longboat

settler

saddle

apoose

knight

Diplodocus

Kingfisher Books, Grisewood & Dempsey Ltd,
Elsley House, 24–30 Great Titchfield Street,
London W1P 7AD

First published in this edition in 1988
by Kingfisher Books.
Originally published in hardback in 1978
by Purnell Books.

This 1989 edition published by Derrydale Books
distributed by Crown Publishers, Inc., 225 Park
Avenue South, New York, New York 10003.

Cover design by The Pinpoint Design Co.
Printed and bound in Italy

ISBN 0-517-69615-0

    h  g  f  e  d  c  b  a

# IT'S FUN FINDING OUT ABOUT

# LONG AGO

## DEBORAH MANLEY

### ILLUSTRATED BY
### COLIN AND MOIRA MACLEAN
### KAILER-LOWNDES AND SALLY GREGORY

DERRYDALE BOOKS
NEW YORK

# Contents

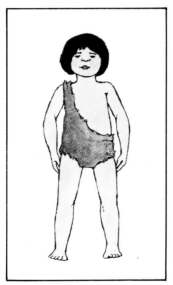

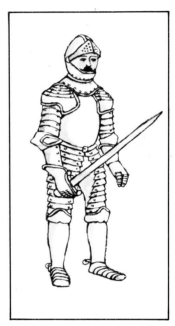

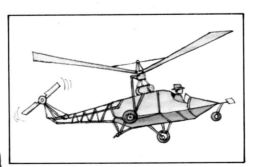

# The world of dinosaurs

Long, long ago, long before people lived on Earth, great reptiles called dinosaurs lived here. You can see from the picture how huge they were.

Stegosaurus had a spiny back to protect itself.

Diplodocus was the longest land animal that ever lived.

Some dinosaurs were quite small.

Tyrannosaurus ate smaller dinosaurs.

The size of present-day creatures

giraffe

horse

man

6 feet (2 meters)

8 feet (2.5 meters)

19 feet (6 meters)

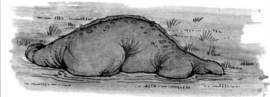

Pteranodon had wings made of skin.
It could glide in the air.

Plesiosaurus lived
in the sea and
hunted fish.

When this Tyrannosaurus
died it fell into
the mud.

After a long time mud
and stone covered its
bones. The bones
turned into fossils.

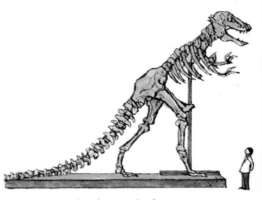

People found the
fossils.
They rebuilt the
Tyrannosaurus.
They put it into
a museum, so many
people can see the
dinosaur
fossils.

# People who lived in caves

Long, long ago people lived in caves.
They hunted wild animals. They made
clothes from the animal skins. They
cooked and   ate the meat of the animals.

They made
boats from
logs.

## How a caveman made tools

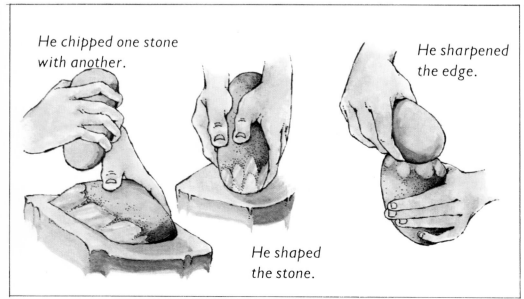

He chipped one stone
with another.

He shaped
the stone.

He sharpened
the edge.

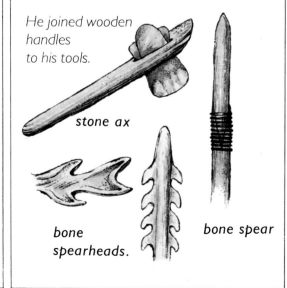

He joined wooden
handles
to his tools.

stone ax

bone
spearheads.

bone spear

Some cave people painted pictures on the walls of their caves.

## Cave people's jewelry

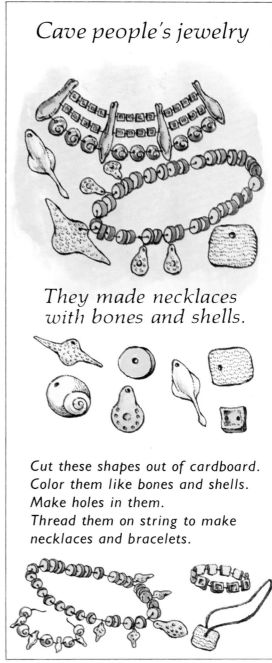

They made necklaces with bones and shells.

Cut these shapes out of cardboard.
Color them like bones and shells.
Make holes in them.
Thread them on string to make necklaces and bracelets.

# How cave people made clothes

They scraped skins clean.

They made holes in the skin.

They fastened pieces together.

# The pyramid builders of Egypt

In Egypt long, long ago they built huge pyramids.
They made the pyramids of stone. They buried
their kings and queens inside the pyramids.

They carved out great blocks
of stone.

They measured the blocks
and cut them to the right size.

They pulled the blocks
to the site of the pyramid.

They carried the huge stone blocks
down the river on boats.

They pulled the blocks
up long earth ramps.

With the blocks of stone
they built the huge pyramids.

# Life in Ancient Rome

The Romans were great builders.
They were great soldiers too.
They conquered many lands.

Romans built temples for their gods.

An aqueduct carries water.

A villa to live in.

a litter

a chariot

Romans built long straight roads.

A Roman book

Roman numbers

1 2 3 4 5 6 7 8 9 10
I II III IV V VI VII VIII IX X

# The Roman army

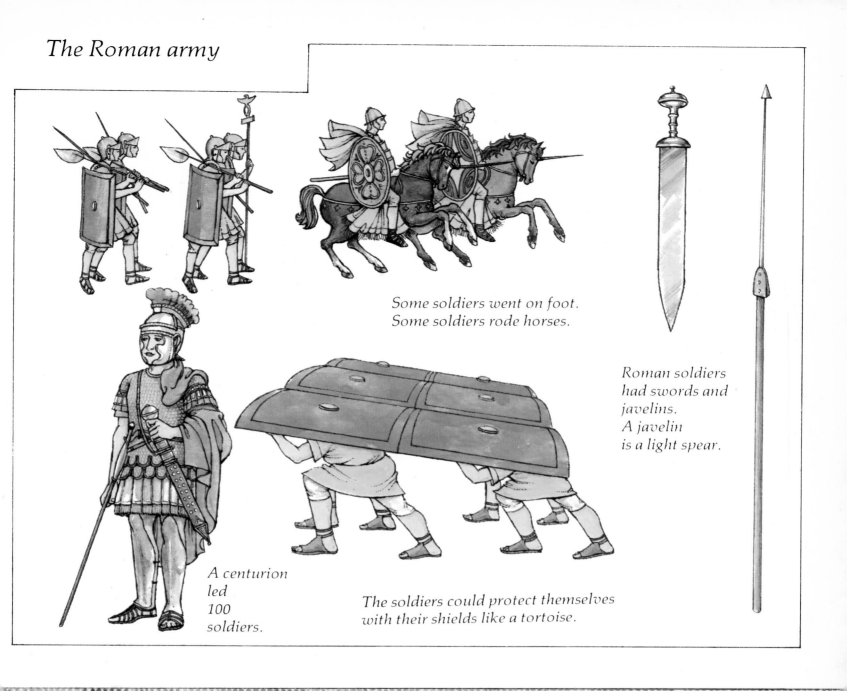

Some soldiers went on foot.
Some soldiers rode horses.

Roman soldiers
had swords and
javelins.
A javelin
is a light spear.

A centurion
led
100
soldiers.

The soldiers could protect themselves
with their shields like a tortoise.

# Making a mosaic

You need:
colored paper
cardboard
scissors
glue

Cut the paper into scraps.

Romans decorated
their floors with
pictures made with
little bits of stone.
These pictures
are called mosaics.

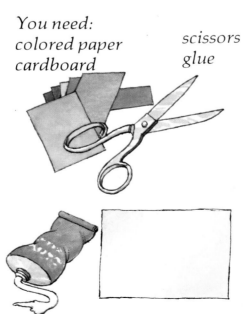

Glue the scraps on the cardboard to make a picture.

# How people measured

This man is using
stones to count.
Each stone is one sheep.

The Chinese used a frame
of beads to count. It was
called an abacus.

The Incas tied knots
in rope to help them count.

## Other ways people counted

on their
fingers    4

with
sticks    6

cutting notches
in wood    8

making marks
on the ground

How many does
this show?

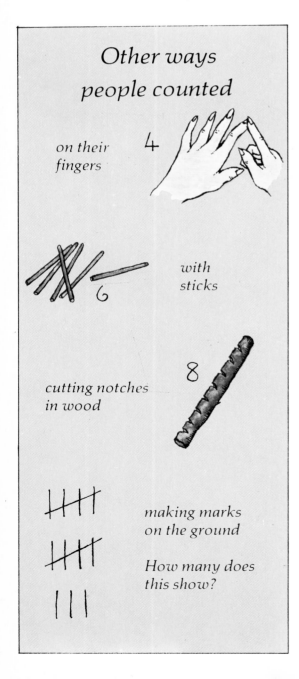

## People used parts of their bodies for measuring.

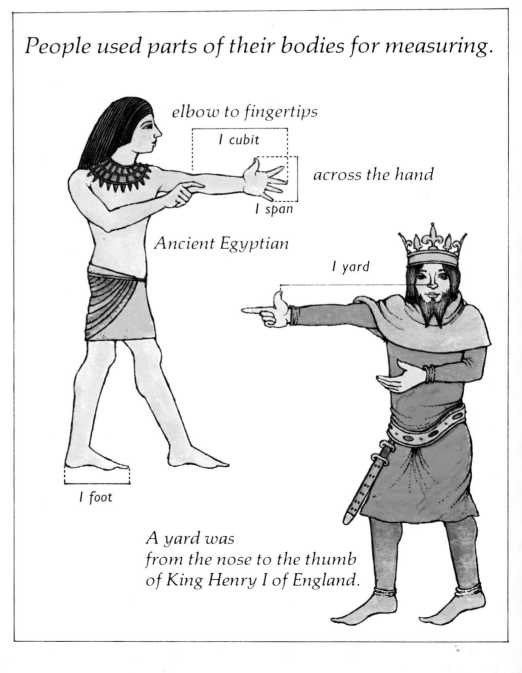

elbow to fingertips

1 cubit

across the hand

1 span

Ancient Egyptian

1 foot

1 yard

A yard was
from the nose to the thumb
of King Henry I of England.

# Measuring time

A candle clock took one hour to burn from one mark to the next.

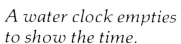

A water clock empties to show the time.

The sun's shadow tells the time on a sundial.

The sand took one hour to drop through an hourglass.

# Make a water clock

Take two paper cups. Make a tiny hole near the bottom of one cup.

Put the cups like this in a bowl. Fill the top cup with water.

Put a mark inside the cup at the water level. Make a mark every quarter of an hour as the water goes down. Fill the cup again. Measure time with your water clock.

# A sun clock

Put a long stick in the ground. Mark where its shadow falls at different times. Tomorrow, look at your sun clock to tell the time.

# Make a candle clock

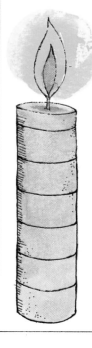

Mark lines around a candle. How long does it take to burn between each mark?

# When Vikings roamed the seas

The Vikings sailed across the sea in their longboats.

A Viking settlement

building a hut

making clay pots     making metal weapons

They attacked other countries.

Then they settled in them.

Make Viking jewelry

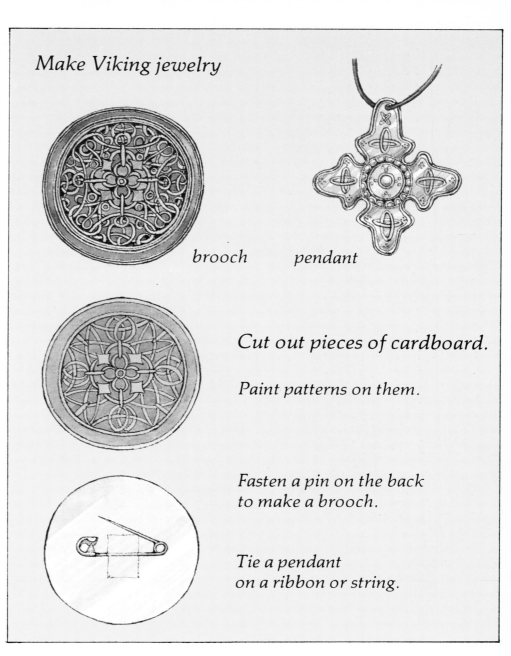

brooch    pendant

Cut out pieces of cardboard.

Paint patterns on them.

Fasten a pin on the back to make a brooch.

Tie a pendant on a ribbon or string.

Everyone lived together in the big house.

# Long ago in China

The Chinese built a great wall around China to keep out their enemies.

The Chinese invented many things.

They invented fireworks.

They made kites.

They made painted china.

They made silk cloth. They painted pictures on silk.

The Chinese ships were called junks. They sailed to many lands.

## The Chinese people wore beautiful clothes.

This is an actor.

child

silk robe

woman

fan

man

bow

helmet

soldier

sword

Chinese writing is different from ours. It is written downward. The letters are painted with a brush.

Chinese people eat with chopsticks.

Find two straight sticks. Can you pick up your food with them?

# People who lived in castles

lord   lady   children   steward   serving woman   knight   soldiers   servant

Long ago these people lived in a castle.
They lived there to be safe from their enemies.

Here is the castle they lived in.

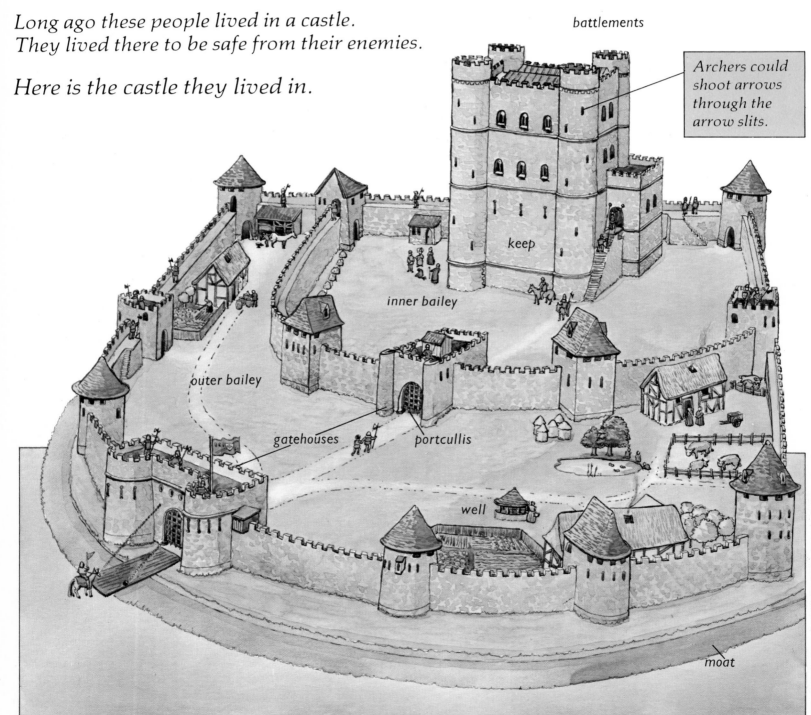

Archers could shoot arrows through the arrow slits.

battlements
keep
inner bailey
outer bailey
gatehouses
portcullis
well
moat

# The lord and his family lived in the keep.

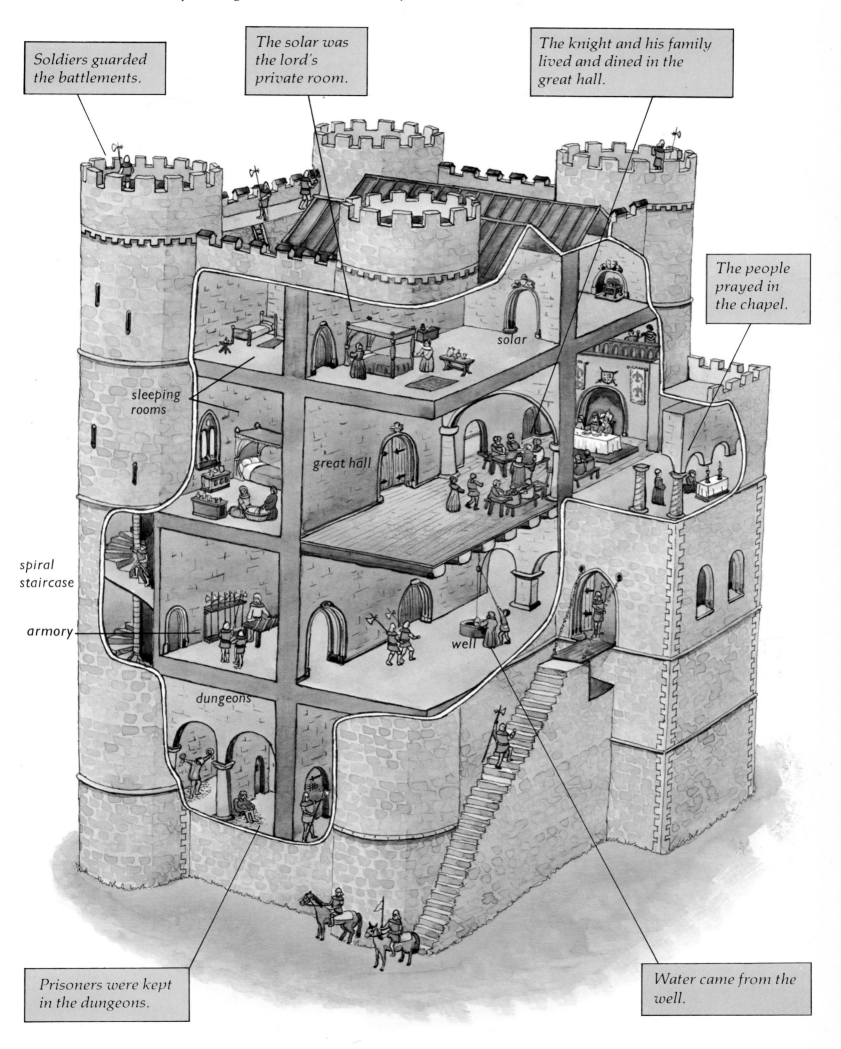

Soldiers guarded the battlements.

The solar was the lord's private room.

The knight and his family lived and dined in the great hall.

The people prayed in the chapel.

sleeping rooms

solar

great hall

spiral staircase

armory

well

dungeons

Prisoners were kept in the dungeons.

Water came from the well.

# Knights in armor

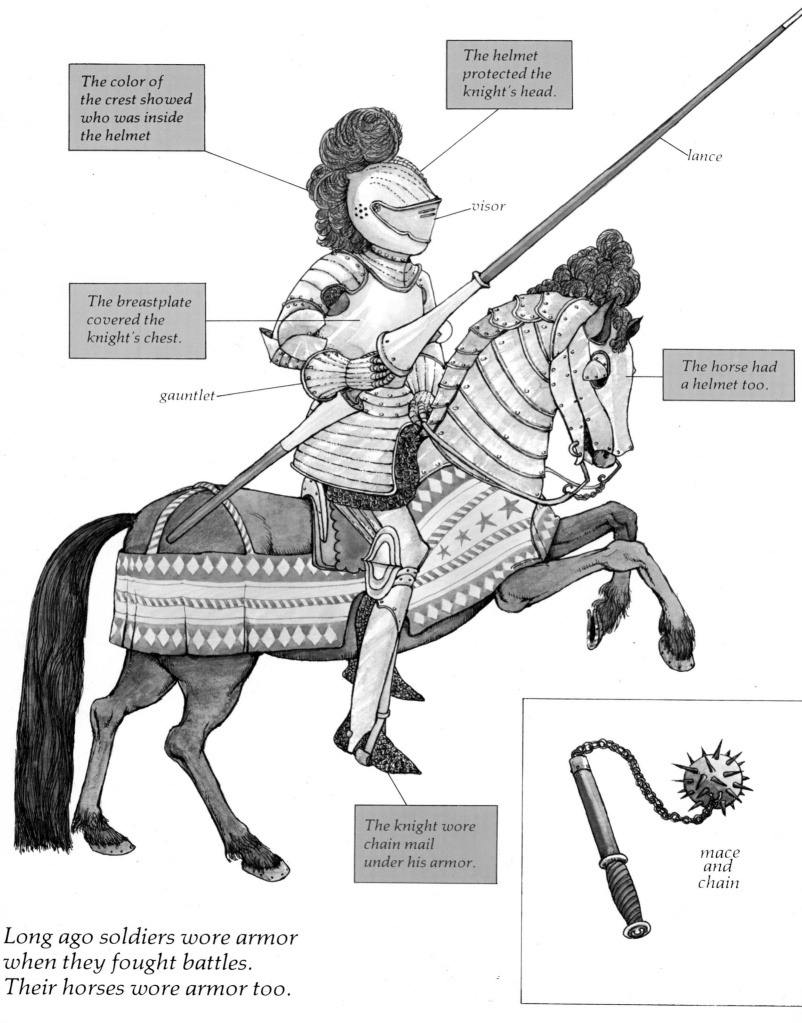

The color of the crest showed who was inside the helmet

The helmet protected the knight's head.

lance

visor

The breastplate covered the knight's chest.

gauntlet

The horse had a helmet too.

The knight wore chain mail under his armor.

mace and chain

Long ago soldiers wore armor when they fought battles. Their horses wore armor too.

A knight could raise the visor on his helmet.

How chain mail was made

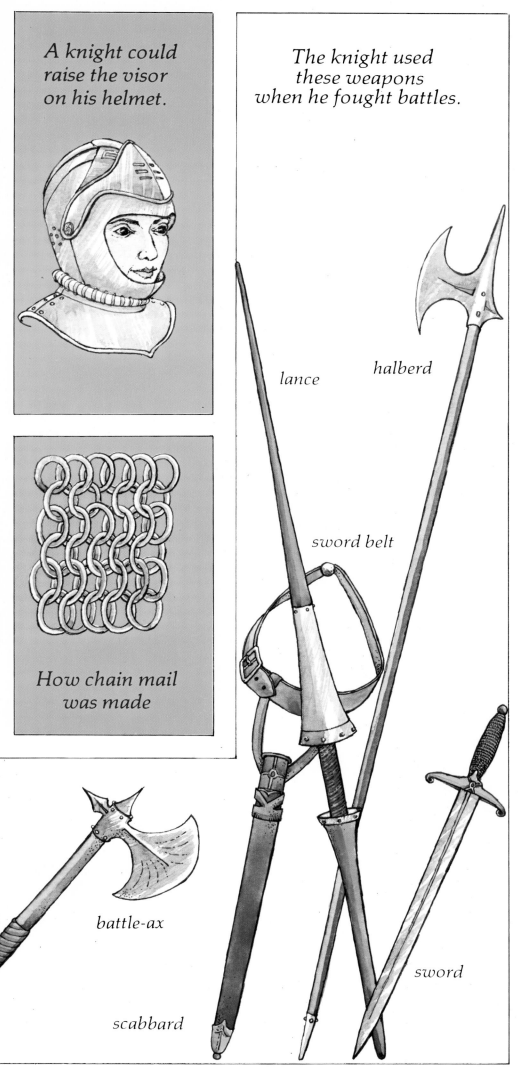

battle-ax

scabbard

The knight used these weapons when he fought battles.

lance

halberd

sword belt

sword

How to make a shield and sword

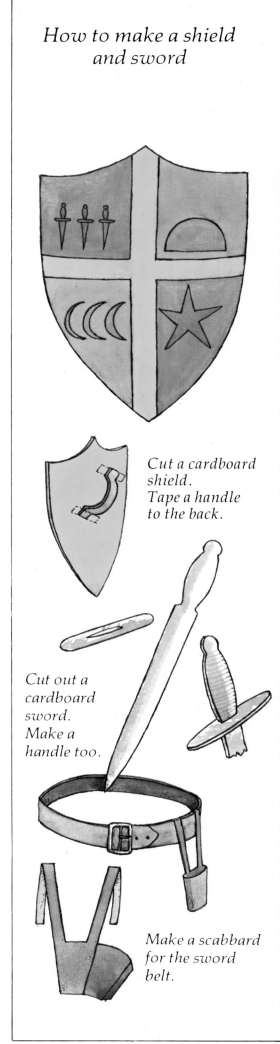

Cut a cardboard shield. Tape a handle to the back.

Cut out a cardboard sword. Make a handle too.

Make a scabbard for the sword belt.

# Ships of long ago

People have paddled and sailed across water for thousands of years.

Cavemen paddled dugout canoes.

Coracles were made of skin.

This man has put a sail on his raft.

Egyptian river boats were made of reeds.

This Egyptian boat could go to sea.

The Romans steered this ship with an oar.

The Vikings crossed the oceans in their longboats.

East Indiamen carried cargo between Asia and Europe.

Clipper ships went very fast.

The Greeks had slaves to row their galleys.

Christopher Columbus discovered America in a ship like this.

Spanish galleons had three masts.

This ship used steam power to cross the Atlantic in 1838.

Use a walnut shell for the hull.

Put a piece of modeling clay inside it.

Cut out a paper sail. Attach it to a toothpick.

Place the sail into the clay in the shell

Sail your boat.

Try different shaped sails.

# Farming in the past

Long ago people had no machinery
to help them on their farms.

Oxen pulled the plow to dig the ground.

The farmer sowed
the seeds by hand.

The farmer cut the wheat with a sickle.

Farming today

A tractor
pulls the
plow.

A tractor pulls
the seeder.

The farmer took the wheat on a wagon
to the windmill.
The windmill ground the grain to make flour.

When all the wheat was harvested, there was a party.

A combine harvester
cuts the wheat.

A tractor carries
the straw.

# Food from long ago

People used to eat all sorts of
strange food.

Knights in castles ate
*whole baby pigs, roast swans,*
*and stuffed peacocks.*

A whole ox would be
roasted on a spit
over the fire.

People eat all these things!

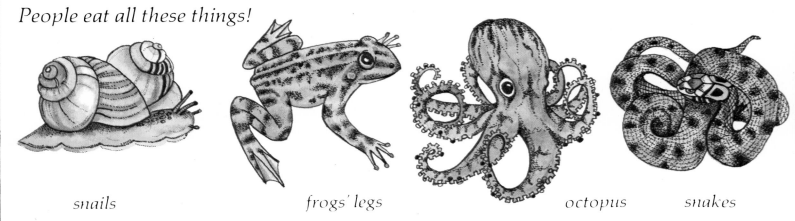

snails          frogs' legs          octopus          snakes

## Christmas pudding

The pudding mixture was tied in a cloth and cooked.

The pudding came out round.

## Pemmican

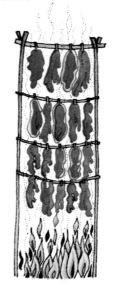

Hunters dried meat over a fire so it would last on their long journeys.

They made it into cakes. It was called pemmican.

crabs          lobsters

People used to have much bigger meals long ago.

oranges

cherries

cake and pies

cookies

turkey

carrots

artichokes

game pie

cauliflower

onions

fish

*Food for a dinner party.*

# The American Indians

Long, long ago only American Indians lived
in North America.
There were many different tribes of Indians.
Here is a camp of a tribe of Indians
who lived on the Great Plains.

These Indians lived
in tepees.

papoose

skins drying

The pony is hobbled
to keep it from straying.

The women made
clothes from skins.

## Some Indian tribes

Navaho

Iroquois

The
Haida
people
built
totem
poles.

Sioux

Apache

32

sending smoke signals

hunting buffalo

The soldiers
and hunters
were called
braves.

The Chief
in his
feather
headdress.

## Sign language

When one tribe spoke
to another tribe,
they used sign language.

friend

buffalo

tepee

peace

horse

trade

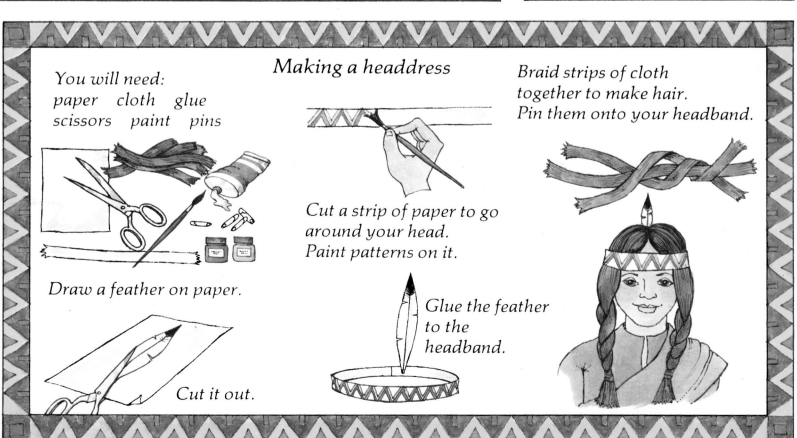

## Making a headdress

You will need:
paper   cloth   glue
scissors   paint   pins

Braid strips of cloth
together to make hair.
Pin them onto your headband.

Draw a feather on paper.

Cut it out.

Cut a strip of paper to go
around your head.
Paint patterns on it.

Glue the feather
to the
headband.

# Settlers and Pioneers

Long ago people left Europe.
They came to live in America.
They were looking for a better way of life.

They had to work very hard.
They cleared land to make their farms.
They built houses with logs.
Can you see the woman making candles?

*Inside a cabin*

spinning wool

cleaning a gun

*Going west*

## The settlers discovered these things in America.

potatoes

tobacco

turkeys

corn

tomatoes

More and more people came to live in America.
They were looking for rich farm land.
Sometimes they traveled right across America.
They carried everything with them in wagons.
Sometimes the Indians tried to stop them.

# The days of the cowboys

Cowboys looked after cattle on the wide open plains of the West.
The cowboy's horse was very important to him.
It took him everywhere.

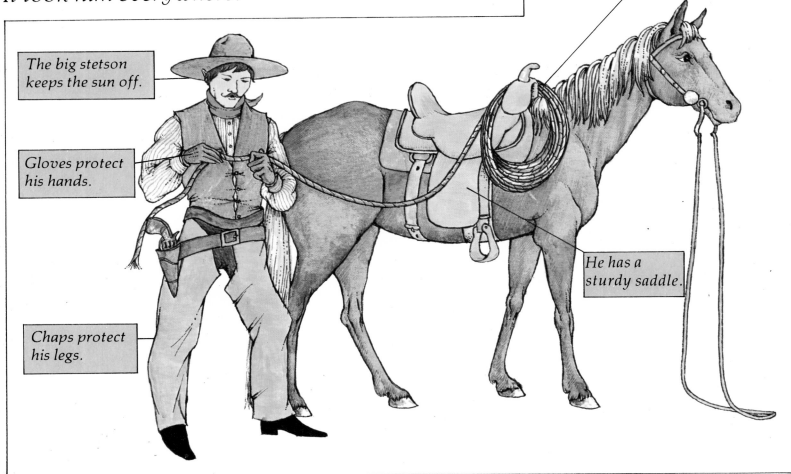

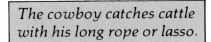
The cowboy catches cattle with his long rope or lasso.

The big stetson keeps the sun off.

Gloves protect his hands.

Chaps protect his legs.

He has a sturdy saddle.

## Back at the ranch

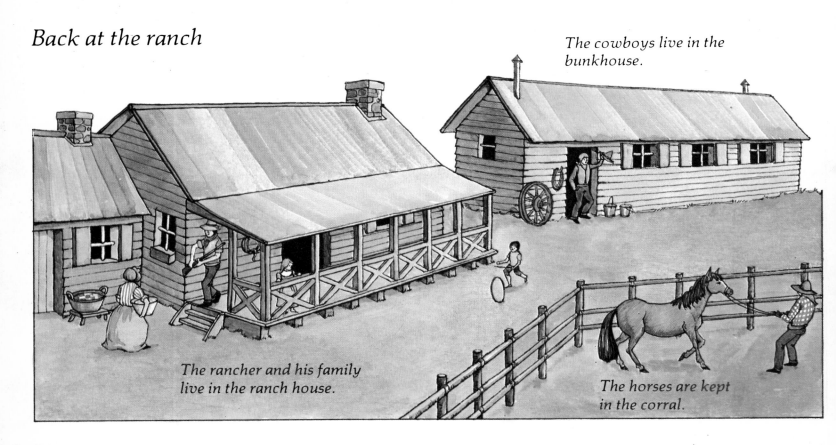

The cowboys live in the bunkhouse.

The rancher and his family live in the ranch house.

The horses are kept in the corral.

# Out on the range

The cattle roamed wild on the prairies.
Each ranch marked its own cattle with a brand or mark.

This cowboy is catching a calf
with his lasso.

The brand is burned onto the calf
with a branding iron.

Here are
some brands.

Rocking A          Swinging M          Lazy 8          Star R

The cowboys rounded up the cattle
to take them to market.

The chuck wagon
carries the
cowboys'
food and water.

# Machines long ago

We have a lot of machines in our homes.

When these machines were invented.
they looked very different.

Here are some of them.

This woman is using a vacuum cleaner.

This woman has to scrub the floor.

This washing machine was turned with handle. The water was wrung out of the clothes with a mangle.

How things have changed

The first tea-maker:
When the alarm went, a match lit a lamp.
When the water boiled, the kettle tipped the water into a teapot.

1902

Tod.

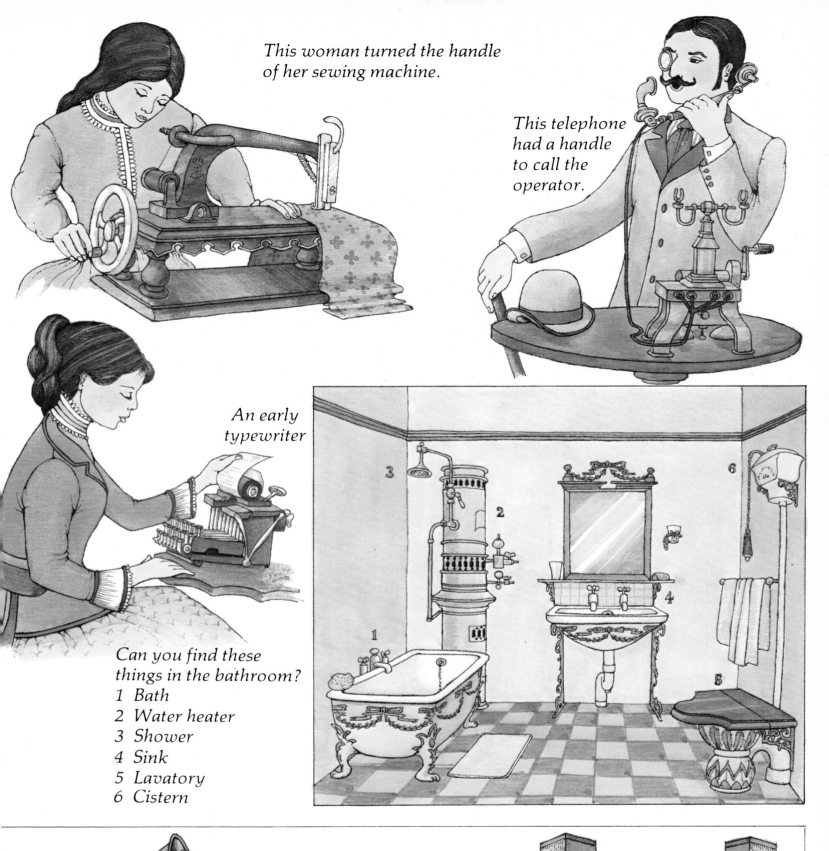

This woman turned the handle of her sewing machine.

This telephone had a handle to call the operator.

An early typewriter

Can you find these things in the bathroom?
1 Bath
2 Water heater
3 Shower
4 Sink
5 Lavatory
6 Cistern

This gramophone or record player had to be wound up with a handle.

1900

Today

# The story of transportation

Cave men had to walk.

Later people tamed horses.

An ox pulled a cart with wheels.

A mail coach
1830

A hobby horse
bicycle
1817

A steam road carriage
1858

Model T Ford
1908

Sports car
1970

Citroen 1938

Stephenson's Rocket 1829

A royal carriage.

The Benz car had
a gasoline engine.
1899

A train in 1900

Engine 1935

Electric locomotive

A Japanese
monorail
train

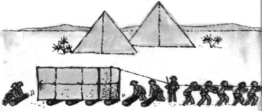

Pulling a load on rollers
is easier than pulling it
on the ground.

Wheels make it even easier.

A pulley helps
to lift things.

Wheels can
turn other
wheels.

Gear wheels
work the
inside of
a clock.

Car wheels
have tires.

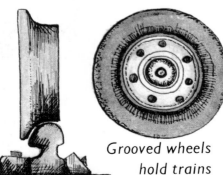

Grooved wheels
hold trains
on a track.

41

# The story of flight

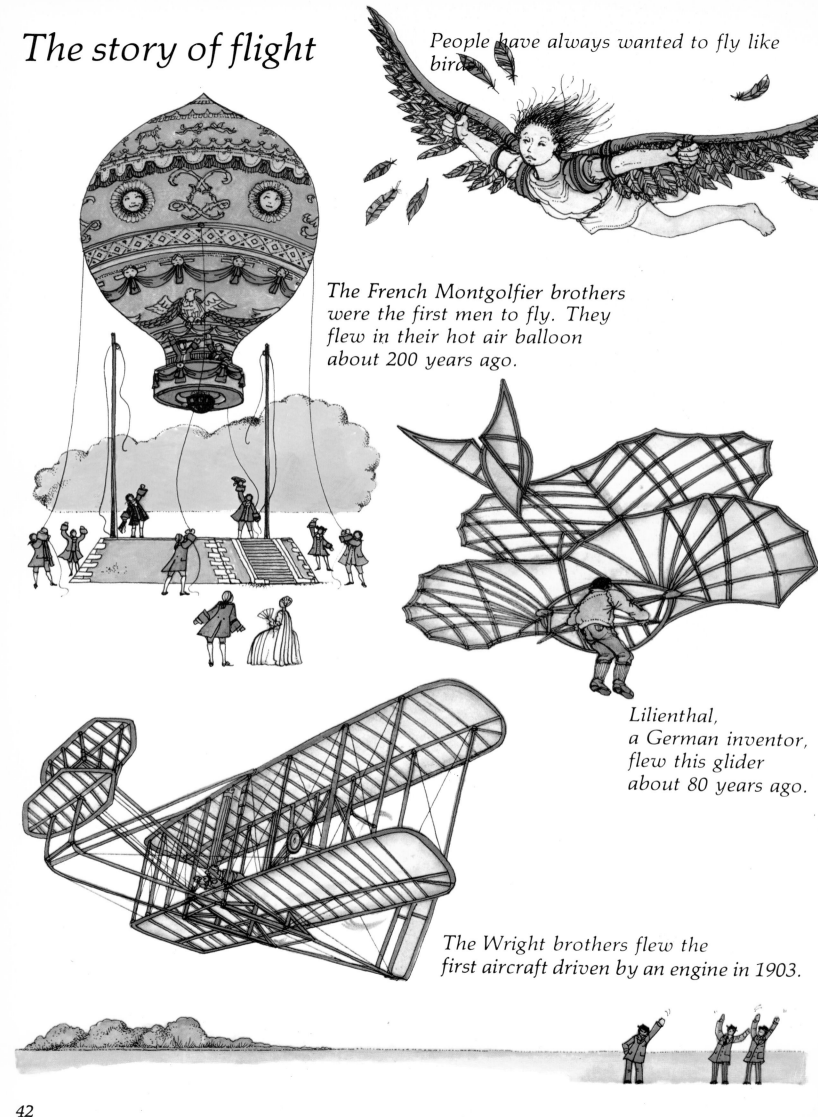

People have always wanted to fly like birds.

The French Montgolfier brothers were the first men to fly. They flew in their hot air balloon about 200 years ago.

Lilienthal, a German inventor, flew this glider about 80 years ago.

The Wright brothers flew the first aircraft driven by an engine in 1903.

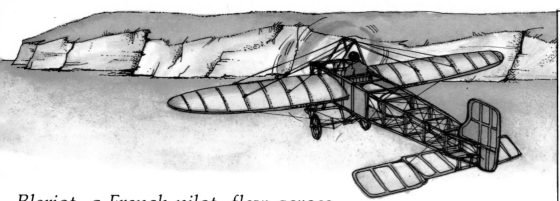

Bleriot, a French pilot, flew across
the sea from France to England in 1909.

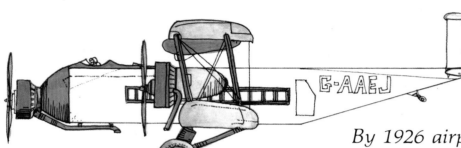

By 1926 airplanes
were taking people
all over the world.

The first helicopter
was flown in 1940.

Huge jet planes carry
hundreds of people around the world.

## How to make a paper glider

Fold a piece of paper
in half.

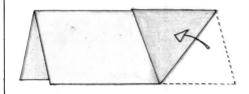

Fold the ends up
on both sides.

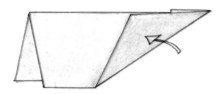

Fold both sides up
again.

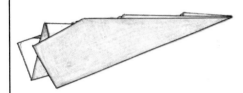

Fold the sides up for
a third time.

Turn the glider over
and it is ready to fly.

43

# It's fun finding out

**What are these? If you do not know,
the numbers tell you which page to look at.**

9

16

24

31

32

19

29

14

39

8

10

17

**Find the answers to these questions.
The numbers tell you which pages to look at.**

Where did cave people paint pictures? (11)
Where did Egyptians bury their kings? (12)
What did Romans build? (14)
What is a moat? (22)

What is a lance? (25)
What is a longboat? (18 and 26)
Where did tomatoes come from? (35)
What is a stetson? (36)

# Which one does not belong?

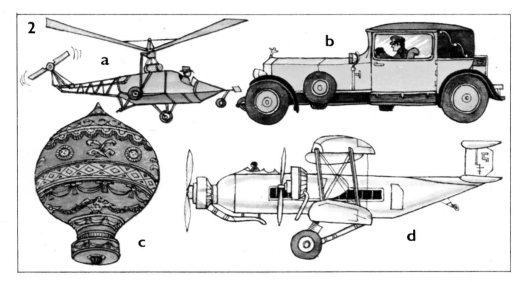

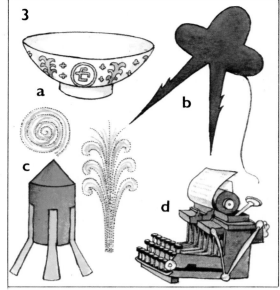

# Who are these people?
## The numbers tell you which page to look at.

Viking

shield

squaw

abacus

pyramid

Christmas
pudding

These
are the pairs:

longboat and Viking
shield and knight
papoose and squaw
Diplodocus and Stegosau
abacus and candle clock
Benz car and driver

cowboy

turkey

Egyptian

stone ax

Roman
book

snails

Chinese
man

driver